MAJORING IN EDUCATION

ALL THE STUFF YOU NEED TO KNOW

RICH HOLLY and LEMUEL W. WATSON

Published by
Meredith Music Publications
a division of G.W. Music, Inc.
4899 Lerch Creek Ct., Galesville, MD 20765
http://www.meredithmusic.com

MEREDITH MUSIC PUBLICATIONS and its stylized double M logo are
trademarks of
MEREDITH MUSIC PUBLICATIONS, a division of G.W. Music, Inc.

Text and cover design: Shawn Girsberger

International Standard Book Number: 978-1-57463-164-7
Library of Congress Control Number: 2011922099
Printed and bound in U.S.A.

Dedication

This book is dedicated to our teachers and mentors. This book is also especially dedicated to those teachers who work from their heart and soul everyday to make a difference in their students' lives.

CONTENTS

acknowledgments

There are several people to whom we owe a great deal of thanks and without whom this book would have been impossible. Our readers, our students, and several of our colleagues have been gracious in providing comments and advice regarding the book, and without their passion for helping us this book would not have been possible. We are deeply grateful to Garwood Whaley for his encouragement, support and savvy insights. Most importantly, we express deep gratitude to Jeanne Holly and Gerard Erley, whose support and love were instrumental throughout the book's preparation. Finally, we acknowledge all of our past teachers who influenced our lives and helped us to see the world full of opportunities. In case we never said thank you, "Thank you!"

iNTRODUCTiON

Congratulations! You may be reading *Majoring in Education: All the Stuff You Need to Know* because you are thinking about majoring or minoring in education, or because you've already made that decision and are about to – or just have – begun your undergraduate career. Maybe you grew up taking care of your siblings and other neighborhood kids and found that teaching was something you enjoyed and that could embrace your creativity and imagination. You might even consider a career in teaching if you enjoyed tutoring, serving as a Sunday school mentor/ teacher, helping coach little leagues, working with a younger boys' or girls' group, baby sitting and other such activities and responsibilities. Choosing to major in education is a noble choice and is likely motivated by your interest in helping children and adolescents learn about themselves and about the world around them. Education is a dynamic field of study and can lead you to many entry level positions in society.

One of the great things about teaching is that no two days will ever be the same. It is a field that is constantly changing and will require you to be a continuous learner. Your students will change every year; new ways of teaching will be introduced for you to try; your colleagues will change from year to year as communities grow; you will have new parents to get to know and partner with each year as well. Consequently, becoming an education major introduces you to a world with endless possibilities to learn about many subjects, but most importantly to learn about yourself and your abilities to grow and develop into a great future teacher.

This book is organized in chapters and sections that will directly address some of the most puzzling questions that you might have about majoring in education. It's important for you to take the time to read each chapter. The knowledge you will gain from this book will save you time and energy during your journey as an undergraduate student and will enhance your success as a college education major.

As you become more acquainted with this book, you can feel more at ease with knowing that you have knowledge that many of your peers may not. You can also be intrinsically excited about your future as a teacher and the influence you will have on your students' lives, their families, your community, and the world.

And most of all, remember to have fun. Yes, that's right, being a great teacher doesn't mean you have to give up the things in life that you love to do. In fact, we believe that you *must* continue to be good to yourself in order to be a great educator.

SECTION I

THE ACADEMIC
STUFF

Time management

Time management is a skill and perhaps an art. As a college student with a goal of teaching, you hone your teaching skills to be better at the art of teaching, so time management is not really that far removed from what you do as an education major. For some readers, time management comes naturally, and for others, you will need to work at it.

Simply put, time management is nothing more than making a promise to yourself that you are going to make time to get everything done to the highest possible level of achievement in the time that is allotted to you. In an academic setting, that usually means both "What am I going to get done today?" as well as "What am I going to get done this week?"

A significant factor in successful time management is learning when to say "No." Sometimes you need to say "no" to yourself, and sometimes you need to say it to others (well, we recommend in those cases you say "No, Thank You."). The majority of students who become overwhelmed with all they have to do, and thus in most cases begin to suffer academically and emotionally, have not yet learned to say "no."

Here's a true story: A young woman, a music education major, was meeting with me (RH) and one of her music professors to discuss why she was not succeeding academically and what she could do in the future to insure better success. She was at a point in her academic career that if she had one more semester like the current one, she would no longer be able to pursue music education as her major. It came out during the meeting that she, in trying to be nice to so many people, was saying "yes" all the time to "Would you play on my recital," and "How would you like to read some duets tonight," and "Can you give me a ride, I have some shopping that I really need to get done," and the like. She was in several ensembles, had a part-time job, and was enrolled in as many credits as one could have without it being termed an overload.

Her music professor and I tried several tactics to try to get her to understand how serious the situation was for her. She had one reason (read: excuse) after another as to why she couldn't say "No" to her friends and change anything in her life. Finally, I said to her, "But you have to realize, that by saying "Yes" to your couple of dozen friends over and over, your status as a music education major is compromised, and consequently you are essentially saying "No" to the thousands of children who would have you as their teacher over the course of your teaching career."

Thankfully, that really hit home with her – her dream was to be a public school music teacher, and she was emotionally distraught at the thought of not being able to attain her goal. She was then able to learn to say "No." She enrolled in fewer courses and ensembles each subsequent semester, and she was able to accomplish all that she originally set out to do, all with much higher grades and greater musical achievement. Now *that's* time management.

Regardless of how naturally organized you might be, there is one helpful tool that we strongly recommend you invest in and use regularly: the day planner. Day planners come in many sizes and forms – from the checkbook-sized, pocketable version to leather-bound versions as large as a binder. There are many popular electronic versions, the Personal Digital Assistant (PDA) being the most common, but also smart-phones and software for your personal computer. All of these, regardless of cost, can get the job done. Most important is that you actually use whichever version you buy.

So, what is it you're going to do with your day planner? There are several things you are going to write down on each day of the current semester: your classes, your clinical observation hours, your meals, any group project time in which you may be involved, and your study time. But here's where it gets really important: every day, you need to do something nice for yourself, and this we like to call "Be Human." Schedule some time each and every day for you to do what it is you like to do that is not school related. It could be taking a walk around campus, playing racquetball, watching "Star Trek" (whichever version you prefer) or playing board games with friends. It doesn't matter what it is – if you like to do it, keep doing it regularly. And keep in mind that as incredible as it may seem, there really is enough time in each day to get done what you need to and what you want to, as long as you have practiced when to say "No" and when to say "Yes."

STUDY HABITS

H ow, when and where you study is typically a personal choice. There is no single method of studying that works for every person. Having said that, there are several tactics you can try. The goal is to have a plan for studying so that it takes the least amount of effort and time with the greatest possible results.

For some of you, you will have developed study skills in high school that work equally well for your college courses. For others, adjustments may be necessary from what you were used to in order to stay "on top" of your college-level work.

When you study is often just as important as how you study. Pay attention to how you feel at different times of the day. You may have a particular time of day that you feel tired, and other parts of the day in which you have plenty of energy. Make sure you schedule your studying for times of the day when your energy is peaking.

Where you study needs to also be considered. At your parents' home, while you were in high school, you likely and automatically retreated to the comfort of the desk in your bedroom to do your studying. If this was successful for you and you can continue this practice in your college dorm room, then we recommend you do that. But you may also find that it's a very different experience. In a residence hall you don't have your own room, your roommate is always talking on the phone, the neighbor's music is coming through the walls loud and clear, and sitting at the desk just doesn't feel right.

If that's the case, we recommend you don't try to make it feel right. Chances are, you can't control either the neighbors or your roommate when you're studying, and trying to do so will just be frustrating for all of you. Instead, take some investigative walks through the campus buildings that you're familiar with – and if you're not yet familiar with both your school's main library and branches, now is the time for that. Most likely in one or more of these buildings you will find at least one spot that has comfortable seating and no one around who might disturb you. This then becomes your personal study place (and don't tell others where it is!). In addition, finding more than one spot to study in may well be your best bet. Recent research has shown that students who alternate their study locations have better retention of the material.[1]

As for the *how* of studying, there are some standard practices for you to try. Some or all may work for you. Find not only a combination of these that works for you, but a particular order of that combination. That will help you stay on track and minimize the time it takes to study.

In no particular order, here are several techniques you can try in order to better remember and understand the material you're studying: re-write your class notes, either by hand or at your computer, which will cause you to give thought to them and perhaps reword them more clearly; highlighting pertinent sentences in your text book for future reference; as you read your notes and textbook, think of questions relating to the material (after all, tests consist of questions, so you'll be giving yourself a mini-test each study session this way);

---

1   Carey, Benedict. "Forget What You Know About Good Study Habits." *New York Times*, 6 September, 2010.

keep a log of your study progress; join with a study partner
or group in order to assist each other; and develop your
own mnemonic phrases to better remember items (just as
young musicians use "every good boy deserves fudge" to help
remember the pitch names associated with the lines of the
treble clef).

Another technique to keep in mind is to divide your study
sessions into various segments. Musicians have known for
centuries that it's best if each practice session include work on
technique, musical etudes and solos, tone production and the
like. Similarly, athletes' practice sessions include stretching,
cross-training, slow movement drills and full-speed drills. In
your study sessions, don't just concentrate on a single item for
a considerable amount of time – make sure you're breaking up
your total study time with an assortment of objectives.[2]

One important item: if you are having problems with a
particular course, don't delay in getting a tutor. For some
subjects there are also subject-specific study tips. For instance,
if you're struggling in your mathematics course, conduct
an Internet search for "math study tips" and contact the
mathematics department on your campus regarding working
with a tutor and for even more information.

2   Ibid.

aDVi SiNG

All colleges and universities have a system of advising in place. We urge you to keep this in mind: Advisors are there to help you. That's their job. It's critical to emphasize how important it is for you to see your advisor on a regular basis – at least one time every semester to make sure you are enrolling in the correct coursework for the upcoming semester. But many advisors can and will do more for you than just checking to make sure you're on track to graduate. It's a good idea to develop a strong relationship with your advisor so you feel comfortable going to him/her when you have questions that need to be answered.

Perhaps the single most frequent reason students go to their advisor is to drop or withdraw from a course. Each campus has its own use of the words "drop" and "withdrawal," so read your college's undergraduate catalog to learn what difference there may be between the two (on our campus, a drop permanently erases the course from your academic record, while a withdrawal is reported as a grade of W). It might be that you need to see your advisor in order to actually withdraw, or it might be that you need to visit a different office on campus for that. Either way, it's a good idea to discuss the matter with your advisor first. Advisors are trained to speak with you about the pertinent issues related to dropping or withdrawing from a course.

Most significantly, before making a decision to drop or withdraw from a course, you must learn whether or not you need to maintain a full-time course load. You may need to do this if you are covered by your parents' health insurance policy, and you may need to maintain full-time status if you receive financial aid. Your advisor can help you with the details of your school's policies, and can make sure you know where you're going before you trek across campus to the financial aid office to ask questions of them.

It is possible to "self" advise, but we don't recommend it. In our combined 50+ years serving as academic advisors as part of our faculty duties, we have met a very small handful of students who self-advised and were actually able to graduate in four years. All the other students we have met who tried to self-advise found themselves in one of our offices with the same story, which began "Well, I *thought* I was going to graduate this semester but I'm not." Meeting with these students is about the worst part of any advisor's job. In some cases, these are students who have already been accepted to graduate school or have accepted employment as a teacher in a school district. Don't put yourself in that position – see your advisor regularly, and take the courses they tell you to take so that you can graduate at the first possible moment.

campus services

Your advisor can also help you to learn what services are available to you on campus. In addition, you can visit the website of the Student Services (or Student Affairs) division of your college or university to find out what these services are. We'll give you an overview of the types of services you can expect to find. The key is for you to recognize when you need any of these services, and then to actually go there and utilize the service they provide. These services are free of charge to currently enrolled students, and they exist solely to help make your life as a student more manageable.

The service you'll probably use the most is the Health Service. Later in this book, in the "Health" section, we'll discuss withdrawing from courses for medical reasons. Let's hope you don't ever need to do that. But you will get colds or the flu, you may come down with allergies, you may get some cuts or scrapes from a pick-up football game, or you may have some gastro-intestinal problems. Whatever the reason, don't hesitate to use the Health Service – you're entitled to use it, the cost of the visit is paid for by virtue of your student fees and/or insurance, and you need to feel better as soon as possible.

One campus service that is often overlooked is the office that helps students who have learning disabilities. Before we go any further, we want to make sure you understand that learning disabilities have nothing to do with intelligence. We can't and won't try to diagnose through writing this section, but if you consistently have the same types of problems studying, learning, doing well on tests, etc., then it's time you looked into whether or not you have a learning disability.

By federal law, should it turn out that you do have a learning disability, your campus is required to provide academic accommodations to you. It is up to you, however, to request these accommodations from each and every professor you have. We have seen many times that these accommodations work – students' lives are sometimes completely transformed once it's determined what their learning disability is and they start receiving the accommodations for which they qualify. If you suspect in the slightest that you may have a learning disability, contact the office on your campus that can help you with this and begin the process of getting an accurate diagnosis.

Your campus will undoubtedly have a counseling service available. In fact, some of you may have already utilized such a service and understand the value of the counseling service on campus. If you haven't used a counseling service before, I encourage you to use the services of your campus counseling facility when you're having emotional or psychological difficulties. When we meet a student who admits they are struggling emotionally but is thus far unwilling to go to a counselor, one of our favorite things to tell them is "Look, your need for a counselor is the same as a home owner's need for a plumber. You have to have one, you may need to find a second one because you didn't like the first one, but if you don't have one you're ultimately in bigger trouble and it will cost you even more money." If you recognize or even just think that your emotional state is not what it can and should be, don't wait – put this book down and go to your campus' counseling service immediately.

Other common student services include tutoring and workshops to develop stronger study skills, time management, note taking or test preparation skills. Most campuses also have resources for several specific populations, such as a women's resource center and a Lesbian, Gay, Bisexual, Transgender center. In addition, it's common to find resource centers for several ethnic populations, such as a Black Studies center, a Latino center, an Asian center, and the like. Remember, you've already paid for these services and opportunities, so take advantage of them to maintain the joy in your life and be the best student and person you can be.

GET INVOLVED

A t our campus, there are over 200 active student
organizations that are "recognized" by the Student
Association. That means that these organizations
receive funding from the SA for their own activities. Many
departments and schools on campus have additional student
organizations that are not recognized by the SA. Recreation
Services on campus supports nearly 20 intramural sports, and
intercollegiate athletics supports 16 competitive teams. The
Graduate School supports hundreds of guest lecturers each
year. The School of Music presents nearly 300 performances
a year, the School of Art has 6 galleries with ever-changing
work being presented, the School of Theatre and Dance
has a new show just about every other week, and there are
three museums on campus. I just love hearing a student say,
"There's nothing to do around here!"

Studies have repeatedly shown that students who are active
and engaged on their campus will have more academic,
emotional and personal success.[3] Students who are not
involved are making a choice to not be involved. Even if your
natural inclination is to be by yourself, at the very least you
can find some other students who enjoy the same hobby as
you and you can start your own "club."

Clearly, there are plenty of campus activities for you to
consider when deciding upon one (or more) in which to

---

3   Alexander W. Astin, "What Matters in College?" *Liberal Education* 79 No. 4 (Fall 1993) : 2.

get involved. Some will give you experience in a form of government, some will give you experience in education, some will give you experience in other settings for which you have a passion. But what's really great is that all of them will give you experience in team-building and leadership, two of the most desirable traits when a prospective employer considers hiring you.

Many campuses host a day when student organizations set up displays allowing you to speak with several of them in one fairly short period of time. But through the magic of the Internet, most student organizations have information on your campus' website. Discover what the various organizations are about, narrow the field down to those you believe you'll enjoy, speak with a representative of those organizations, and get involved.

SECTION II

THE EDUCATION STUFF

WHaT'S iT aLL aBOUT?

E ducation is really about helping individuals learn for as many reasons as you can imagine. One assumed basic reason for organized, formal education is to produce an educated citizenry to maintain our great democracy and to ensure that we have an educated workforce due to the fact that we are also a great capitalistic society. The most essential reason for education is also to empower individuals to think critically about their own lives, community, and the world in which they live, to give them the tools they need to be empowered to make the world a better place for all.

The field of teaching requires professional training, certification or state licensing, and/or endorsements depending on the roles, levels, and ages you desire to work with. Since teaching is a professional field, there are numerous local, state, regional, national, and international professional associations to help to keep students and professionals up-to-date with common concerns for the profession.

What is a profession? Most would describe a profession as having common philosophy, fieldwork and knowledge-based preparation about a certain field. Typically, professions will include some form of recognition like an endorsement, a license, or a certification which is earned through a combination of practice, knowledge, and testing based on a set of agreed upon general standards. Such strenuous standards also allow teachers to be experts and enjoy a lot of autonomy in working with their students.

In education, the population that you serve changes each year. In most day-to-day environments the populations served are adolescents or younger and are taught as a group rather than individually; certified teachers work with groups, not individuals, in general. All efforts to individualize instruction for any child must be done while simultaneously focusing on the group concerns, and you never know all of the real benefits or affects you have on your students' learning compared to other professions (Lay-Dopyera and Dopyera, 1987).

The relationship that teachers build with children and their parents is therefore short and minimal unless the community and school are small. Also, most teachers do not choose their students to work with; they accept who their students are and work with them. In addition, there are laws that require students to stay in school even though they are not directly in control of how or who serves them. No other profession is quite like the teaching profession where individuals are not directly responsible or involved in determining the services provided. In addition, teachers are directly and broadly responsible for students' well-being while they are in school. The teacher is legally expected to serve 'in loco parentis' (in place of parent or guardian) of students while under school supervision, and to take measures necessary for their well-being. In addition to the legal issues to consider, teachers are frequently faced with the societal or public criticism when it comes to best practices for teachers. Because everyone has been through an education system of some sort, everyone believes he or she knows best about how to teach and to educate. No other profession must constantly deal with everyone telling them how to best do their jobs. The positive perspective from this public discussion is that education is always a priority.

Finally, as a teacher, you will be expected to be many things to many individuals. Remember, a teacher is a social engineer who is engaged in the life of the community in addition to being a teacher. The days are long and include work outside of the classroom, including grading homework, preparing lesson plans, communicating with parents, and a host of other tasks that you determine are helpful to the student and school.

Education as a Field of Study and Profession

I n addition to the basic general liberal arts courses required of all college and university degree programs, most undergraduate education majors are required to complete an introductory course that provides a cursory overview of the development of education in the United States. Most education majors and minors take courses that are offered directly by the faculty of an education department, and most of these courses are always related to pedagogy (methods of teaching), students' development, student assessment, and other education-related courses that would not be taught in other majors (such as history or science). Most education courses have titles such as Assessment in Teacher Education, Foundations of Education, The Culture of School, Postmodern Issues in Education, Diverse Students in the Classroom, Curriculum Development, and development or method courses for the appropriate age group(s) you want to teach. More specific courses deal with curriculum development and techniques for teaching various subject areas and age groups (generally early childhood, elementary, and secondary or adolescent). You might also find some universities that offer a range of courses that are extremely specific to types of schools you would be interested in, from Montessori to Christian, urban to rural, and private to public. Remember that every community has a school, and students need teachers who care about their well-being and development.

As noted above, all majors will have to complete the general education requirements to fulfill the degree requirements for the major/minor and university. General education requirements exist to help individuals gain a broad sense of the world across many subjects, including psychology, sociology, social sciences, history, health, philosophy, political science, English, mathematics, foreign languages, the arts and others. Education majors and minors must also fulfill the requirements of student teaching and field work.

Striving toward a profession in education is a great way to spend your undergraduate years. As far as options for careers with a teaching degree, there are many. Graduates with teaching degrees may go into many fields as professionals. The training that one gets as a major in education could be the basis for work with children, adolescents, and adults in a variety of organizations. However, you need to know that majoring in education is not like other majors because you will spend a significant amount of time learning about teaching methods, child development, and basic assessment methods in addition to spending time in the field. Unlike other majors, you will have to get used to the legal necessities like background checks. It is very important that you prove yourself as a moral and law abiding individual. So, in addition to learning about your major, you will need to learn about the school and classroom setting, and know enough about basic workplace policies and laws to survive in your own classroom. Remember – teaching requires that you use all of your abilities and interests to focus on enhancing student learning and development. It is next to impossible and unethical to do only a partial job in the classroom. You will come to understand as an education major that teaching requires a total personal commitment.

Teaching and education have vastly changed due to government programs that require teachers and schools to demonstrate that students are being taught and that the students are learning. Begun during the George W. Bush administration, the national No Child Left Behind Act (NCLB) and various state programs have required school systems to make significant alterations in education methodology. Most colleges of education are well aware of various accountability issues that teachers face. These schools should be preparing future teachers to deal with state and local measures to ensure students are learning and that teachers are making a difference in their students' learning and development.

What is NCLB? This act requires that teachers have the appropriate credentials and competencies to teach what they have been assigned and to whom they have been assigned to teach. NCLB was the re-authorization of the federal Elementary and Secondary Education Act (ESEA) in 2002. In 2010, under President Barack Obama, ESEA is again being considered for re-authorization. We encourage you to visit the link provided in the "Important Resources" section of this book for more and current information.

Choosing a College and Program

L ooking for a school with the best reputation that trains teachers may be a little tricky. The best advice would be to just ask some of your teachers what school they would recommend. Ask them about their experiences as an education major. If you have a favorite teacher, this conversation would be welcomed by him or her. Even though there may be a major age difference between you and some of your teachers, keep in mind that many teachers continue to go back to college or university during the summer months for additional coursework. They would have a good idea of how helpful most of the faculty and advisors are with their students in the education program of the colleges and universities they've attended. Don't forget that as you prepare your application materials, often your teachers could serve as references for you if they are alumni of the program and institution. Another reliable choice in assisting you with narrowing down your choice is the high school guidance counselor who would have lots of information about which schools have the best reputations for certain education specialties. You may also choose to refer to some of the national periodicals or magazines like Newsweek or U.S. News & World Report rankings. Just remember that although an institution might make the list it does not mean that your major will be of that same quality. Similarly, schools not on the list may have a very successful education program.

As you search for an academic home, don't forget that you need to find the best place that would provide a good aesthetic and social fit for you. It helps to think of this process as an interview for the institution as well. In advance of looking for colleges and universities, determine your priorities in what an institution has to offer. You might want to consider the following questions as you make your decision:

- What are the financial incentives for education majors to attend the institution? Do they offer scholarships in your field of study?

- What is the student to teacher ratio for your major? In other words, how many students will generally be in your major classes competing for the attention of your professor?

- Do the full-time tenured professors, part-time instructors or graduate teaching assistants teach most of the courses?

- Does the college, department, and faculty seem open and welcoming to you? Do faculty seem rushed and stressed or do they speak, smile, and acknowledge your presence?

- What percentage of the school's education majors/ minors pass state certification and licensure exams?

- Do professional and student organizations focused on education majors exist on campus?

- What is the placement rate of graduates from the program, for both teaching positions and graduate schools?

- Do students normally get placed in their student teaching assignments in the semester they request?

- What is the time requirement for student teaching and does the institution provide transportation to and from the school?

- Does the school work well with career placement services to provide a job fair for employers and employees to meet?

- How is student teaching structured? Is it a year-long experience or a semester experience? Is student teaching part of the bachelor's degree requirements or is it an add-on?

- Is the education program a four-year degree or a five-year degree?

One website you might want to become very familiar with as a future teacher is the National Council for Accreditation of Teacher Education (NCATE) http://www.ncate.org/. In fact, NCATE shares helpful hints on what to look for in a college:

- Does the institution offer a firm foundation in the liberal arts and teaching disciplines?

- Are programs designed using subject matter-specific standards developed by specialized professional associations (e.g., the National Council of Teachers of Mathematics, etc.)?

◼ Does the institution have the resources necessary to support each of the programs it offers?

◼ Does the institution prepare candidates to integrate technology into instruction? How well is technology integrated into the coursework at the institution? One course in 'technology' is not sufficient.

◼ Does the institution provide many opportunities for candidates to learn how to teach under the supervision of a variety of veteran teachers? At what point does the candidate gain experience in P–12 schools? Many institutions now offer this experience as soon as possible so that prospective candidates better understand schools from a teacher's point of view.

◼ Does the institution prepare candidates to work with the growing diversity of America's school population?

◼ Do teacher candidates acquire knowledge of the most effective teaching strategies? How are teacher candidates evaluated on their performance by the institution? By whom are the prospective teachers evaluated? How is it accomplished?

◼ What percent of the graduates pass the state licensing exam?

◼ How does the institution seek feedback from graduates, and how is it incorporated into the program? What has been the feedback from graduates?

◼ What has been the feedback from principals, department chairs, etc. at schools hiring graduates? (http://www.ncate.org/public/lookfor.asp?ch=2, accessed September 16, 2010)

We recommend that the college or university you choose to attend be accredited by a national organization such as NCATE or the Teacher Education Accreditation Council (TEAC). Plans are currently underway for NCATE and TEAC to combine into a single accreditation body known as the Council for the Accreditation of Educator Preparation (CAEP).

Activities to Ponder:

1. Make a list of all of the things you are looking for in a college – socially, environmentally, and academically. Make sure you include things like distance from home, the size of the school, in-state or out-of-state. It's also a good idea to make a list of the program traits you are seeking. For example, small and intimate, friendly faculty, team work atmosphere, etc. When you have exhausted the list, circle the top three things you cannot live without. Hold on to those items as you search for your college and program.

2. Ask your five best or favorite teachers what they believe are the top three programs in your area for preparing teachers. See if they all come up with similar answers.

CHOOSING a
major

S o – you've chosen which college or university to attend and the time has come to declare your major. Within the field of education there are several options for you to consider.

Take the time to really think about the things you most enjoy. Think about the subjects you excel at and if you like to work in teams or alone. Find your curiosity and passion so that you could spend thousands of hours talking about the subject matter as well as finding new ways to teach it. Maneuvering through a major requires you to get to know a number of people at your institution. In fact, most advisors (general and major-specific) and career counselors would all be of help if you get stuck in the process. As you narrow down your choice for a major keep in mind your favorite class, your natural talents, what you really enjoy learning about, and if you enjoy sharing that knowledge with others.

Also remember that based on the college or university and the state in which it resides you will have different options regarding how you fulfill the requirements for a major in education. At some colleges, undergraduate education students typically minor or specialize in a specified subject matter in addition to majoring in education. Undergraduate students should try hard to get as much course work in a specific subject matter other than education as possible.

Elementary education majors in some states have to major in a subject and get endorsed (approved) in order to teach the appropriate age group. We hope by now you have an idea of the subject you'd like to minor in if you are going to be a teacher.

As stated earlier, most colleges and universities require students to take prerequisite courses known as general education requirements in a wide variety of subjects during the first two years of college. This would include subjects in the humanities, sciences, and so on. The rationale behind the general education requirements is to introduce you to a broad spectrum of subjects and to broaden your overall knowledge of the liberal arts. You should try to appreciate these courses because they could open a door of opportunity for you to recognize skills, interest, and curiosity in a subject to which you had previously never given a second thought.

If you know you want to major in education but haven't chosen a subject in which to concentrate, consult with an academic or guidance counselor. Counselors often can help you determine which direction to take simply by discussing your likes and dislikes, grades in particular subjects, research papers you've previously written, and your academic predispositions to either humanities or science classes, as well as to elementary or secondary school students.

If you choose to enter an elementary education program, a minor isn't considered necessary in most cases, as most grade school teachers are expected to provide a general overview of such core subjects as mathematics, science, and reading comprehension; hence, the liberal arts (sometimes called "general education," or just "gen eds") become very important. A minor will always help one become more marketable, especially if you have a minor or endorsement in the subject area that is the current national or regional focus.

Activity to Ponder:

Choosing a major goes hand-in-hand with a program and college. You should visit your prospective schools without your parents to see how you are treated as a student. Visit the advising office, clinical placement office, the department office and just sit and observe the atmosphere in the area you believe you want to major in. Walk past the faculty offices as well. How well were you treated by staff and faculty in just passing in the hall ways? Did they greet you with a smile or ask if they could be of help? Did students speak to you? Make a list of your observations and consider if you would be happy and productive in such an environment.

WHAT LEVEL DO I WANT TO TEACH — ELEMENTARY MIDDLE, OR HIGH SCHOOL?

Take the time to seriously think about if you like older adolescents or very young children, because this becomes very important and could save you precious time later. Here's another true story: one student we worked with believed that she wanted to teach early childhood-aged children until she had to spend her first day of internship with them. Good thing she was only a freshman, because she could not take the smell of diapers and did not want to deal with changing them when the little ones had an accident! She was lucky that she learned her limitations early in her academic experience. Think how horrible this situation might have been had she nearly completed a degree in early childhood education before she discovered this about herself. You should give considerable thought to the age group choice. The gender issue will sometimes influence whether a male or female will follow their passion or not. For example, a male who wants to work with young children in early or elementary school would need to know that he will experience some prejudices due to the fact that he is a man who enjoys working with younger kids.

Colleges of education teacher preparation degree programs are organized in the following manner: they prepare individuals to teach children of the early childhood years (often birth to early elementary school grades); kindergarten through sixth (or sometimes eighth) grade; or secondary school (both middle and high school). The elementary education program has commonly added on pre-school requirements and has become focused on preschool through sixth grade in most places. Again, this would depend on various state requirements and certification and endorsement rules and regulations. You must remember that institutions of higher education are required to align their programs with their state's license requirement so that program graduates are prepared to ensure the minimal quality expected (Miller, 1979).

Activities to Ponder:

1. Ask your top five teachers why they chose to teach at their current grade level.

2. Take the time to visit a class for each level if possible. Spend enough time in the classroom to really find out how morning, noon, and afternoon might be different.

3. Did you find more joy in observing one grade level more than the others? Why do you think that is?

Tests and Certification

The licensing or certification of elementary and secondary teachers in the United States is a state responsibility. The regular route for licensing teachers is through the approved university's education program or department. This process means that a college or university submits a plan for a teacher preparation program for each subject area and/or grade level(s) which adhere to each state's guidelines for approval. Therefore, most teaching certification candidates apply for their teaching certificate directly through the college- or university-approved routes. The university is responsible for making sure all requirements are met before processing the paperwork and sending it to the state. All requirements would include passing all tests, health and background checks, student teaching, and required coursework. In the event that the student does not meet all requirements, he or she may continue to work on areas that need improvement or choose to major in another discipline. For example, some students have a really hard time passing the first test, called Basic Skills or Praxis I. This is a test of basic knowledge information that high school students should easily pass. We highly recommend you take it as soon as possible after high school graduation.

Many programs will require that you pass the basic skills test or Praxis I before you are fully admitted to the program or if you come into the university as an undecided major.

The content knowledge test or Praxis II is about the specific content area and other education-related questions. Students may take the various parts of the test all at once, or test for the different parts of it separately. At many institutions, students who do not pass this test may not pursue a degree in education or certification. In this case, students may decide to get a bachelor of general studies degree if the institution offers such a route. Please remember that requirements for obtaining a license to teach through approved program routes vary enormously, not only from state to state but also from institution to institution.

Some states require passing different and/or additional tests as well as requiring differing lengths of time in student teaching. Some require observation in schools before student teaching. Some institutions of higher education have added a "fifth year" to their teacher education programs. Others have added internships. Others have done away with undergraduate teacher preparation programs altogether, and just have a post-baccalaureate program of teacher preparation. In these programs, students finish a bachelor's degree in some academic field and then return for a fifth year to focus on education coursework and field experiences.

Some states require only the initial certificate; other states require a second or even a third stage certificate – sometimes with continuing education requirements and sometimes resulting in a life or permanent certificate. "The terminology used for various types of teaching licenses is terribly confusing. There are different titles used for the initial teaching certificates, and more titles used for the second stage teaching certificates throughout the 50 states and the District of Columbia. Emergency certificates have been the age-old means of bringing individuals quickly into teaching. Some states wanted to develop an alternative to such emergency routes." (http://www.ncei.com/Alt-Teacher-Cert.htm; accessed September 16, 2010)

Again, various states require multiple tests and different tools for assessing the competencies of their teachers. We refer here to NCATE's simply-described phases for becoming a teacher:

■ Phase 1:

Preservice preparation is the first step toward becoming a teacher. By attending an accredited school of education, you will gain a foundation of knowledge about teaching and learning as well as opportunities to practice teaching your chosen subject under supervision. The teaching profession's accrediting body is the National Council for Accreditation of Teacher Education (www.ncate.org). After receiving your undergraduate degree, you will need more professional development (Step 2) to gain the complete set of knowledge and skills necessary to succeed in the classroom.

■ Phase 2

Earning a beginning license, commonly known as a novice license, is the second step to becoming a teacher. In most states you must pass a test of subject matter knowledge and sometimes an additional test of pedagogical knowledge. The novice license will provide you with an opportunity to start teaching for a designated period of time. In addition, you may also be required to go through a mentoring program or attend professional development activities before earning your professional license.

More and more states are now using a tiered licensing system which includes mentoring programs and extended clinical practice (such as professional development schools). This system helps provide beginning teachers with the support and assistance they need to become successful and to help ensure that they will continue teaching after their first year.

The process described above is not unlike what beginning professionals in nearly all other fields experience as well! Practitioners in established professions must first gain a foundation of knowledge by graduating from a professionally accredited profession. For example, after graduating from a preparation program, engineers, social workers, and psychologists must work under supervision for a lengthy period before being awarded a professional license.

■ Phase 3: Advanced Certification and Career Development

Professional teachers must keep up with advances in the field throughout their career and engage in continuing professional development to broaden their knowledge and skills. Successful teachers continuously work on improving their teaching ability reviewing research and available data on student achievement to find out which teaching methods work. For career advancement, advanced certification is available to teachers through the National Board for Professional Teaching Standards (www.nbpts.org). Certification incentives include formal recognition, a larger salary, and leadership opportunities.

The three phases of teacher preparation and development above correspond to three quality assurance mechanisms for the field: professional accreditation; state licensing; and advanced certification. All established professions use these mechanisms to assure public trust in the professionals who are licensed to practice.

Every state requires that teachers in public schools be certified by their departments of education as being qualified to teach; some states require certification for teachers in private and parochial schools as well. Certification differs by state, and each state has its own certification process and home office. You'll need to check the certification requirements in the state you'll be teaching in for more detail. To locate the correct office in your state, start with such terms as The State Department of Education or State Board of Education. For example, in Illinois the title of the organization is the Illinois State Board Education. In South Carolina, the organization is the South Carolina State Board of Education. Just conduct an Internet search for "teacher certification" and you will most likely find what you need (Horowitz and Walker, (2005).

Activities to Ponder

1. Discuss with your favorite five high school teachers what continuing professional development they're engaged in. Why did they choose those subjects or activities? Are their professional development experiences meeting their expectations?

2. Ask your teachers to describe how confident (or nervous!) they were during their initial classroom observations or clinical experiences. What did they learn from those experiences?

STUDENT TEACHING

Every education major and minor knows that he or she must go through the experience of student teaching. It is impossible to become a certified teacher without this apprenticeship. It is a time of reflection and an excellent opportunity to hone your skills. By the time you reach your student teaching experience, it is hoped that you know the types of students you are interested in working with and the subjects you hope to teach, even various pedagogy and classroom management techniques that you can lean on during the most challenging of times. Let's all hope there will not be any surprises! If you are diligent in your program of study and really want to excel at teaching, you would have spent enough time in schools during your four or five years in your program, starting with your freshman year to the culminating experience of student teaching.

Each state will have a minimum amount of time that you must fulfill in student teaching in order to earn your state certification. Some university education departments will have requirements beyond that of the state they're in. You need to be prepared to do a number of activities during your student teaching experience. Also, your program might be set up with para-professional seminars which provide students with opportunities to discuss their experiences with their peers and supervising faculty as well as to discuss various professional concerns, requirements, and so on.

Before you are assigned to a student teaching placement post, you will have to work with your department's, college's or unit's clinical placement office or clinical placement person. These placement professionals are responsible for acting like the broker between you and the school. Most placement professionals are very knowledgeable about the schools they have partnered with for students' placements. They are also keenly aware of those teachers who have been good role models and fair with pre-service teachers or student teachers. If you haven't done so sooner, you should make every attempt to get in touch with the clinical placement professionals at your institution at the end of your junior year or before the semester you start your student teaching. It is your responsibility to know all of the deadlines and to get your application for placement in as early and correctly as possible. As noted earlier, you will need to make sure all of your legal requirements are completed and processed by the required deadlines in addition to completing your academic requirements.

Next, you need to make sure you get to know your cooperating teacher and your supervising teacher. Cooperating teachers are the individuals you will be working with on a daily basis in the schools; it is his or her classroom and students that you will be responsible to teach. The cooperating teacher is expected to model for you and to mentor you through the process, and it's important that you develop a respectful relationship with this individual. The supervising teacher is the college professor or instructor who works with you and the cooperating teacher to work out issues, concerns, or challenges. Supervising teachers will be the first individuals to know if there are problems or concerns with your performance. You should be respectful of this relationship as well.

When it comes to discussing your student teaching experience, let's start with the most challenging issues first.

One must be ready for the unthinkable: after all of your commitment and at the end of your student teaching experience, you might then come to the discovery that you really do not want to teach. Our suggestion at this time would be to make an appointment with your academic advisor to discuss alternatives for obtaining your degree. We mentioned earlier that one could seek a general studies degree if your institution offers such a degree. Remember, there continues to be many career options open to you with a bachelors degree in general studies. It's also very likely that your institution offers other degree programs that would suit your needs.

If for some reason there are problems between you and your cooperating teacher, you should involve your supervising teacher after you have respectfully tried to understand the problem. You should also make sure you know the policies and rules and regulations of your college and department in case there are unsolvable issues. In any case, feel free to contact the administrator of the unit (dean, chair, head) if your supervising faculty member does not help remedy the situation. The administrator would be the individual to work directly with the principal of the school should a need arise. The best advice is to not quit and remember that it is only for a short time in the big scheme of things.

Starting off a good relationship with your cooperating teacher might be as simple as just meeting with him or her at their school prior to the first officially scheduled meeting. Keep in mind that most of the individuals who are cooperating teachers have lots of experiences and many times are not as excited as you might be. In fact, some cooperating teachers may have two or three university students who are in and out of their classes in one year. Some of these university students might be completing internships, while others might be helpers who are getting familiar with the context of the school. You'll be competing for your cooperating teacher's time and attention in cases such as these. So, at least offer to meet earlier, in advance of the semester, to become familiar with your cooperating teacher, what topics you will be teaching, what text books you will use, and, if possible, information about your students and their backgrounds. Ask for as much detail as possible without putting too much pressure on the teacher. You might ask about lesson plans with dates and if you could have a weekly meeting to discuss your performance and tips to enhance your teaching and classroom management techniques. You will also score points if you offer to help with any other appropriate duties, such as mentoring, tutoring, evaluating exams or papers, and the like.

Some professionals recommend that students get to know other teachers and administrators around the school. We believe it depends on the individual. However, we can say that networking is generally a positive endeavor that leads to positive outcomes. Being friendly, professional, competent, and optimistic are the traits that most individuals like to have in a colleague and in an employee. These characteristics will also be helpful when you meet the parents of the students. Get information about the parents ahead of time if possible. If you will be introduced to parents, work with your cooperating teacher with regard to how you are introduced to them.

Please act as though school truly matters to you and that it is not a burden during your field experiences. In other words, don't let anyone hear you complain about anything in your school. Although you might have other duties to attend to at the end of the day, don't be a clock watcher. Leave school patiently, not rushing to get out of the building. Perceptions are important and they matter during your student teaching and later as a practicing professional.

Be realistic about all of the multiple factors that are involved in the experience that no one can control. Be reasonable and rational with your expectations and your approach to success with field experiences. Give yourself enough time to reflect on your daily activities and don't be too hard on yourself.

Activities to Ponder

1. During your semester of student teaching, stay in touch with other student teachers with whom you're friendly. How did their week go? What challenges did they have, and how did they work through them?

2. Keep a journal of your daily work as a student teacher. Take special note if you experience the same successes or challenges frequently. Share these observations with your supervising teacher.

Yes, There are alternative routes to the classroom

A s deans, we have seen the power of alternative routes to certification in our region. It is an option for many individuals who are career-changers and also a reasonable tool for school districts to use to find qualified teachers who care about their communities. With the onset of alternative certification programs in the United States, traditional programs in colleges of education have to adjust to be competitive since the alternative route is market driven. One great item that we have seen is the seriousness given to the field experience and how important it is to have pre-service teachers get in the classroom sooner and stay there longer so that one understands the context of the school and community.

According to the National Center for Education Information (NCEI), the term "alternative teacher certification" historically has been used to refer to a variety of avenues to becoming licensed to teach. In addition, NCEI has been polling state departments of education annually since 1983 regarding alternatives to the traditionally-approved college of education program route for licensing teachers. They found that both state and individual providers of alternate route programs have increased with attention being given to some standardization.

In 2005, 47 states, plus the District of Columbia, reported 122 alternative routes to teacher certification being implemented by 619 providers of individual programs around the country (NCEI). NCEI has conducted a study on individuals entering teaching through alternate routes to certification and can be found at www.ncei.com and www.teach-now.org.

Clearly, alternative routes to teaching are bringing non-traditional populations of people into the teaching profession who want to help young people develop and teach where the demands for teachers are greatest. More specifically, individuals are attracted to the alternative teaching route because the program is designed with them in mind. These programs are designed to meet the demand for teachers in geographic locations and in subject areas where the demand for teachers is greatest; in addition, programs are specifically designed around the community context. Generally speaking (from the NCEI website):

- Programs are specifically designed to meet the preparation needs of individuals who already have at least a bachelor's degree and, in many cases, experience in other occupations, to teach in specific areas and in specific subjects.

- Programs are job-specific. Rather than train people to teach who may or may not ever go into teaching, alternative route programs recruit individuals for specific teaching positions and place prospective teachers in those jobs early in their training programs.

- The teacher preparation program is field-based.

- Prospective teachers work with mentor teachers while teaching.

- Candidates usually go through their program in cohorts, not as isolated individuals.

- Most of these programs are collaborative efforts among state departments of education whose responsibility it is to license teachers, colleges and universities that historically have had the responsibility for educating and training teachers, and school districts that actually hire teachers.

If you're interested in pursuing an alternative route to teacher certification, we recommend you visit the "Important Resources" section of this book to find more information.

And, speaking of alternatives, there is one other teaching career you may consider – that of a college or university professor. While it's beyond the scope of this book to describe the various considerations you need to know about becoming a professor, we will say that we need excellent, dedicated and passionate teachers at all levels. If you have a burning passion to teach a specific subject area, or even sub-topic, you might consider doing so at the collegiate level. If this interests you, we recommend you speak with your current professors, administrators and advisors to learn what you need to know about becoming a professor.

Final Thoughts about Teaching

Whatever you might decide about teaching, remember that it is one of the very most important, essential and noble professions one may choose to follow. Teachers are necessary and are creators of our next great generation and world. A teacher has the capacity to light a fire under any pupil towards his or her destiny; hence, a teacher has the ability to cause a wild fire through their students. You should not forget that somewhere in some school in some classroom our best and brightest were taught by a teacher who cared enough to keep and fan the flames of hope and optimism for individual students to believe the unbelievable.

There is no other profession in the world where you get to control and create your own world through creativity and innovation while passionately engaging others to join in the journey. We can promise you that no two days will be the same and that you will experience life to the fullest through your peers and pupils.

SECTION III

THE LIFE
STUFF

EMBRACING a POSITIVE ATTITUDE

I f there is only one thing you take away from having read this book, knowing that you need to develop and maintain a positive attitude is that one thing. This trait will serve you well – indeed, very well – your entire life, no matter what directions your life and career take.

The power of a positive attitude has been well-documented. Generations were raised knowing the effects of "The Power of Positive Thinking" by Norman Vincent Peale (Prentice-Hall, 1952). Anthony Robbins is a one-man international star and corporation because of his positive attitude and ability to instill that in others. An entire industry – motivational speaking – has thrived based on how effective a positive attitude is.

Perhaps you've noticed – throughout this book we've used the words "joy" and "passion" several times. This is why we teach. This is why we play music. This is why we mentor. And when you do something that you greatly enjoy, when you *play*, it brings with it a warm, good feeling. You have the ability to turn that personal, warm feeling into a positive attitude and keep it with you wherever you go and in whatever you do. And we also believe you have an obligation to share that attitude with those around you.

Perhaps you've heard this "light bulb" joke before: How many people does it take to change a light bulb? Ten. One to change the bulb, and nine to stand around saying, "Big deal. I could do it better than that." The one changing the light bulb likely has a positive attitude and the nine standing around and criticizing clearly have bad attitudes.

If a teacher or organization advisor asks for a volunteer, do you jump at the chance to be the one "changing the light bulb?" Or do you prefer to sit back and criticize the volunteer? When a classmate is having difficulties with an assignment, do you stay quiet and relish in the thought that you're not having difficulties? Or do you gently assist your classmate with helpful tips on how to better understand the material?

We're reminded of two great examples of using a positive attitude to create something extremely powerful. The first is when music producer extraordinaire Quincy Jones recorded "We Are The World" (Columbia Records, 1985) with a bevy of international stars in order to raise funds for drought-stricken Ethiopia. Jones was questioned about how he was able to get so many big name singers to work together so well in such a short period of time to make such a successful recording. He stated that at the entrance to the recording studio, he taped a sign saying "check your ego at the door."

The second example is the 2008 U.S. Olympic basketball team. For many years, this team was nicknamed "The Dream Team," due to the roster being completely populated with NBA stars. In 2004, however, the team did not live up to its billing – 10 of the 12 original players bowed out prior to the Olympics, forcing the U.S. to find last-minute replacements. That year's team lost more games than any other U.S. men's basketball team. However, because of that year's team, USA Basketball sought players who would make a three-year commitment culminating in the 2008 Olympics. Because several high-profile players decided to "check their egos at the door" and play for the U.S. team for three years straight, the 2008 Olympic team brought home the gold, winning all of its games by a nearly 30-point average.

As a professional educator, no matter which grade level you prefer to teach or if you move into an administrative post, you will be a member of a team. To be at the top of your game, you need to know how to work as a team member – how to maintain and use that positive attitude at all times. As a teacher your attitude will rub off on your students. As an educational administrator those around you will notice and react to you based on your attitude. Some of you will find yourselves as an employee of a large corporation where you'll be speaking and meeting with dozens of people each and every week. Your attitude will determine how far you get in your field, regardless of which specific field you're in.

Howard Schultz, the famed CEO of Starbucks who built the company from a single store to the international corporate giant it is today, says it beautifully: "Success should not be measured in dollars: It's about how you conduct the journey, and how big your heart is at the end of it."[1] When you teach, lead and interact with others, remember and feel the joy, and let your positive attitude steer you in the right directions.

---

1   Howard Schultz and Dori Jones Yang, *Pour Your Heart Into It: How Starbucks Built a Company One Cup at a Time* (New York: Hyperion, 1997), 337.

HEALTH

Undoubtedly you've heard this said but we'll say it again: Your health is the most important thing. This is not just some time-worn cliché, it is the truth. And let's be clear: in this section, the words "health" and "medical" are referring to both psychological as well as physical health.

As university administrators, one of our duties is to speak with students who are unable to attend classes due to health problems. Some semesters it astonishes us how many students are in this situation. But even more troubling are the students who ignore the tell-tale signs of sickness and convince themselves that they will magically get better on their own.

We can tell you – utilizing that philosophy is *not* in your best interest. What happens in all too many of these cases is the student's health deteriorates further, they cannot continue to attend classes and complete the coursework, and their permanent university record displays low grades.

All colleges and universities have a system for withdrawing due to medical reasons. If you are unable to attend class due to medical reasons, it is very important to get an early diagnosis and subsequent treatment from a physician, either at your campus health service or through a private practice. We also recommend you contact your advisor very early on in order to discuss your withdrawal options and the procedure you must then follow.

Your overall, general health is of the utmost importance. As was discussed earlier in the Study Habits section of this book, you may find that you are tired at a re-occurring time each day. If you have more than one time each day in which you feel tired, then we recommend a trip to your physician, getting more exercise, getting more rest/sleep, changing your diet, or some combination of these.

It's important that you engage in some form of exercise on a regular basis, which can be as simple as a long walk several times a week or as regimented as weight-training and/or aerobics sessions every day. It can also be through your participation in an intramural sport, or frequent biking, rollerblading, jogging, softball with friends, etc. It doesn't matter what it is – what does matter is that you find a physical activity you like and make it part of what you do on a regular basis.

Getting enough sleep is often overlooked by college students, but it is an essential part of your overall health. The National Sleep Foundation (www.sleepfoundation.org) recommends that going to bed at a similar time each night, getting 7-9 hours of sleep, and waking up at a similar time each morning will provide you with enough sleep so that you function at your fullest capacity.

One of the phrases that's commonly discussed is the "freshman fifteen." This refers to college freshmen and women gaining fifteen pounds. Although recent research has shown this to not be true, it can be true that maintaining a nutritionally sound diet may be difficult.[2] Additionally, most

---

2   Carole Nhu'y Hodge, Linda A. Jackson, and Linda A. Sullivan, "The 'Freshman 15': Facts and Fantasies About Weight Gain in College Women," *Psychology of Women Quarterly* 17 (1993) :119.

nutritionists agree, it's just as important that you eat three balanced meals a day. Pay attention to what and how much you're eating. To be alert numerous hours a day in classes, observing in schools, group project sessions and study time, you need to be in good health.

roommates

As a student in most colleges and universities, you will be assigned a roommate by the staff of the campus housing office. How they determine who will live with who is a great mystery. For some roommates it works out beautifully, for others it can be a horrible experience. Of course, we hope that your roommate and you get along well and can coexist without any problems. But if you are having problems, you must do something about it.

Each campus will have its own policies and regulations for how you go about switching roommates, so you need to inquire about those policies so that you understand what your options and rights are. Before you pursue moving out of your assigned room, we encourage you to speak with the residence hall staff and/or the university ombudsman, all of whom are trained to assist with conflict resolution. The ombudsman's job is to help facilitate communication and if necessary mediate a resolution between members of your college or university. Seeing your ombudsman is free of charge, and rest assured they will help you in a completely confidential manner to find a workable solution to your roommate problem. Working out the differences you and your roommate are experiencing may be all that you need.

CHOOSING
FRIENDS

O ne of the greatest things about being a college
student is all the wonderful people you will
meet, many of whom will become friends for life.
Unfortunately, there are some college students who are
not so wonderful and may be inclined to commit crimes
(obviously, stay away from them). There are some college
students who are well-intentioned but are "high maintenance"
and having a relationship with them will eat up all your
time (be honest with them and tell them you cannot spend
that much time with them). There are also students who
are having psychological problems and may come to you for
solace. To best help these friends, you might consider walking
them over to your campus counseling service so that they
receive professional help.

Think about the friends you had in high school. Most likely,
you had much in common with them in terms of likes and
dislikes (music, fashion, sports, politics, religion, chess,
what have you). But also think about your friends' level of
dedication to their studies and ability to focus. If you can
honestly say that your high school friends had the same
dedication and focus as you, which we hope were both high,
then you already have a good track record of choosing friends.

We meet regularly with students who tell us they are not
getting their work done because their friends constantly

pressure them into joining them in some social activity, and the student feels obliged to go with them. If this is the case with you, then it becomes very important that you tell your friends that you're not getting your school work done and you need to study and work on your assignments more. If they are really your friends, they will understand and you'll see no difference in the way they treat you. If they have a problem with you being honest with them, and become negative, then perhaps they are not the best choices of friends for you.

money

Personal finance expert Suze Orman says that money is the number one reason why couples argue. Health and wellness educator Terra Wellington reports that for the majority of people, money and finances are two of the most stressful factors in life. And according to a 2004 survey administered by the American Psychological Association, almost 75% of those who responded claimed that money was the number one cause of stress for them.

Of course, in college, you have tuition, room and board expenses, student fees, the cost of text books, project supplies purchases, other potential supply needs based upon your course work, and a desire and probably a need for weekly spending money. To be honest, about the last thing you need in addition to your course work and studying is to have financial worries.

Some of you will have all your education-related costs paid for by your parents. On the opposite end of the spectrum, some of you will be working part- or maybe even full-time in order to pay your school expenses. And some of you will work hard and for long hours in the summers so you can save money to have while you're at school the other 9 months of the year.

Here's another true story: One of our students decided it was time to join a rock band, get some experience doing that, and make money while he was at it. The band he joined rehearsed 40 miles away from our campus. The student had to buy a car in order to get to these rehearsals and ultimately gigs.

In the meantime, to pay off the loan on the car, he had to take a job at a fast-food restaurant working 20-25 hours a week. He began eating 2 or more meals a day in the fast food restaurant.

So, literally overnight, here was a student who went from having a week consisting of a full-time course load, rehearsals for two school ensembles, private practice time and study time, to a schedule that included all that *plus* 20 or more hours a week of work, 15 or more hours a week driving to and from and the playing in rehearsals and/or gigs, and eating most of his meals in a not very nutritionally sound manner. As you may have guessed, his school work and personal practicing went completely downhill, he gained a great deal of weight, and was constantly overstressed.

What this student failed to do was to seriously consider how the money came into play in his decision to join that particular rock band. To him, he was making a decision about an experience he wanted as a musician. While that's partially true, what he had also done is turn his finances completely upside down and subsequently his studies and health, as well.

What we hope you learn from this is that before you agree to add something to your life as an education-related major, you need to take some time to think through whether this decision will positively or negatively affect your financial situation. Just because you may make some money on the side doesn't mean that in the big picture it's good for your pocketbook, or, as in the case above, your health and well-being. The same consideration is for those of you working to pay your school bills. You need to seriously consider how many classes/credits you can successfully carry in a semester if you are working at a job so many hours each week. Do yourself a favor, and remember, as we discussed in the Time Management section, to say "No." Don't overdo it.

Then there's the financial aid part of the equation. Many of you will be receiving financial aid in order to pay your college expenses. Financial aid comes in three basic forms: talent or academic scholarship awards, grants, and loans. By the time you are enrolled in courses, you and your family will likely know what your financial aid package will be and will begin to make plans to pay for your education.

The federal government, in conjunction with state governments, enforces a group of policies that govern not only who qualifies for financial aid to begin with, but also how a qualified student *remains* qualified semester after semester. On many campuses, this is referred to as financial aid Satisfactory Academic Progress (SAP) or Reasonable Academic Progress (RAP). Each campus may develop its own system of dealing with students who do not meet SAP/RAP status, but there are a few generalities you should know.

In order to remain eligible for financial aid, you will likely need to (1) maintain at least a 2.00 Grade Point Average, (2) pass more than 2/3 of your courses, and (3) have attempted no more credits than what would be 150% of the total credits required for your degree program. If you are a student receiving any kind of financial aid (and that means about 70% of you), we strongly urge you to contact the financial aid office on your campus if you have any questions regarding your financial aid package, your eligibility, or any other related issue.

ALCOHOL AND DRUGS

The legal drinking age in all 50 of the United States is 21, and the peer pressure to drink alcohol before age 21 is often very strong. And although they are illegal substances, you will likely meet students who encourage you to use drugs.

Most (and possibly all) college campuses have help for students with questions or concerns about alcohol and drugs. Before you make a decision whether or not to drink alcoholic beverages or use illegal drugs, it's a good idea to understand the answers to your questions and to gather as much information as possible. Check your college's website for this kind of information, or contact the Student Affairs office on campus. You need to be fully informed about the legal ramifications as well as the physical and psychological effects drugs or alcohol would have on you, and make sure you understand your campus' policies before you make a decision. We encourage you to keep in mind this simple and true statement: *one poor choice can ruin your life.*

We can tell you that every year, students leave college due to problems with drinking alcohol and/or using drugs. Very few things are sadder for us than to see a talented, intelligent young student either be academically dismissed from school or have such serious health problems that they must leave school due to their drug or alcohol use.

Virtually all students come to school very excited about their college career and what the future holds for them, and if the wrong decisions are made, that future can be put in jeopardy. We can't tell you what to decide, but we will encourage you to speak with your parents, speak with a counselor on your campus, speak with a member of the clergy or speak with an older relative you admire. Be informed, and make smart decisions so that one day, we can count you among the vibrant members of the professional educators' world.

sexual relations

Perhaps this topic is just as difficult as alcohol and drugs, but you must, at the very least, think about it. Understanding the topic of sexual relations is important for all students regardless of sexual orientation. By now, we hope you know that if you do choose to have sexual relations while in college, you need to have protected sex, whether you are gay, straight, or bisexual.

But there are additional issues you need to know about and be ready to make decisions about. Do you understand what consent to having a sexual relationship means? Do you know the many definitions of rape? These definitions refer to more than only penetration by a man to a woman. Rape and sexual assault are defined by law, and consent (or lack thereof) is a defining factor in rape situations. Have you determined and are no longer struggling with your own sexuality? Do you understand what sexual harassment is? What effects might drugs or alcohol have on your sexual relations? Are you prepared for the ramifications of you or your partner becoming pregnant?

Be aware that college and university campuses are not immune to cases of domestic violence, date violence, stalking and cyber stalking. While not always of a sexual nature, these instances do often result from a relationship into which you

entered. Make sure you really know the person you are with before committing to a sexual relationship.

Thankfully, your campus will have resources available to help you learn the answers to these questions and to help you make the best decision you can for yourself and even for your partner. It's in your best interest to be fully informed before you decide about sexual relations for yourself.

Be Good To Yourself

Here's something else that is true: you must be good to yourself if you wish to succeed. We'd like for you to keep two things in mind. First, your college transcript (the official recording of your grades) follows you for the rest of your life. You need to have it look as good as possible for those jobs or graduate schools you may apply to that require one. And second, college graduates often get hired based on the level of achievement and leadership they can demonstrate either through a portfolio or resume (also known as a vita, or curriculum vita, or C.V.).

To have your transcript look good or even great, and to be the best job candidate you can possibly be when you graduate, you need to be good to yourself. Eat correctly, get some exercise, get enough rest, deal with stress, be smart about alcohol and drugs, get help when you need it, ask lots of questions, and don't be in a rush to graduate. Many of you will indeed graduate in four years, but many of you will take five years to complete your program. It doesn't matter to an employer or a graduate school how old you are when you graduate. They're looking for the best educator with the best transcript and best level of maturity and responsibility. So if staying in school one more year will help either or both your level of teaching skills or the grades on your transcript, then we would encourage you to strongly consider taking that extra year to earn your degree. And remember: you made

a noble choice to become a teacher. Now get out there and show the world what a terrific influence you can be.

resources and references

important resources

To learn more about No Child Left Behind and the proposed re-authorization of the Elementary and Secondary Education Act, visit the U.S. Department of Education at http://www2.ed.gov/nclb/landing.jhtml.

To find out more about the Praxis I test, which is administered by Educational Testing Services, visit the Praxis website at http://www.ets.org/praxis.

The National Council for Accreditation of Teacher Education explains the steps necessary to become a highly qualified and effective classroom teacher, available at http://www.ncate.org/documents/CurrentFutureTeachers/TeacherContinuum.pdf.

To learn more about alternative routes to classroom teaching and certification, there are several helpful websites, including the following:

Troops To Teachers

http://www.dantes.doded.mil/dantes_Web/troopstoteachers/index.asp

National Center for Alternative Certification

http://www.teach-now.org/

Teach for America

http://www.teachforamerica.org

National Center for Education Information

http://www.ncei.com/Alt-Teacher-Cert.htm

references

"As Tax Deadline Approaches Americans Say Money is
Number One Cause of Stress" [Article, March 31, 2004].
American Psychological Association Press Release.
Available from http://www.apa.org/releases/moneystress.
html. Internet. Accessed 5 July 2006.

Astin, Alexander W. "What Matters in College?" *Liberal
Education* 79 No. 4 (Fall 1993) : 4-16.

Basco, Monica Ramirez. *Never Good Enough: Freeing
Yourself from the Chains of Perfectionism.* New York: The
Free Press, 1999.

Carey, Benedict. "Forget What You Know About Good Study
Habits." New York Times [Article, September 6, 2010].
Available from http://www.nytimes.com/2010/09/07/
health/views/07mind.html?ref=general&src=me&pagew
anted=all. Accessed 8 September 2010.

Chickering, Arthur W. and Zelda F. Gamson. "Seven Principles
for Good Practice in Undergraduate Education" [Article,
March 1987]. *American Association for Higher Education
Bulletin.* Available from http://www.csueastbay.edu/
wasc/pdfs/End%20Note.pdf. Internet. Accessed 5 July
2006.

Gille, Susan V. "The Influence of Social and Academic
Integration and Use of Campus Resources on Freshman
Attrition." Ph.D. diss., University of Missouri-Kansas City,
1985.

Hodge, Carole Nhu'y, Linda A. Jackson, and Linda A. Sullivan. "The 'Freshman 15': Facts and Fantasies About Weight Gain in College Women." *Psychology of Women Quarterly* 17 (1993), 119-126.

Horowitz, J. A., and Walker, B. (2005). "What can you do with a major in education?" *Real people. Real jobs. Real Rewards.* New Jersey: Wiley Publishing, 2005.

Lay-Dopyera, M., and Dopyera, J. (1987). *Becoming a Teacher of Young Children* (3rd Ed.). New York: Random House, 1987.

Mallinger, Allan E. and Jeannette De Wyze. *Too Perfect: When Being in Control Gets Out of Control.* New York: Clarkson Potter, 1992.

Malone, Michael S. *The Everything College Survival Book* (2nd Ed.). Massachusetts: The Everything Series, 1997.

Miller, H. L. *Choosing a College Major: Education.* New York: David McKay Company, Inc., 1979.

Orman, Suze. "Five Remedies for Couples who Argue About Money" *Yahoo Finance.* Available from http://biz.yahoo.com/pfg/e39couple/art021.html. Internet. Accessed 5 July 2006.

Psychology Today Staff. "Perfectionism: Impossible Dream" [Article, May/June 1995]. *Psychology Today.* Available from http://www.psychologytoday.com/articles/pto-19950501-000002.html. Internet. Accessed 14 June 2006.

Rodriguez, Nancy C. "Success at School: Get Involved Beyond School" [Article, August 1, 2004]. *The Courier-Journal.*

Available from http://www.courier-journal.com/cjextra/
backtoschool/2004/stories/p11_activities.html. Internet.
Accessed 5 July 2006.

Schultz, Howard and Yang, Dori Jones. *Pour Your Heart Into
It: How Starbucks Built a Company One Cup at a Time.*
New York: Hyperion, 1997.

"Sexuality" *Harvard University Health Services.* Available from
http://huhs.harvard.edu/healthinformation/sexuality.htm.
Internet. Accessed 5 July 2006.

Starr, Raymond. "Teaching Study Skills in History Courses."
The History Teacher 16 No. 4 (August 1983) : 489-504.

"Understanding Financial Aid." *College Summit & National
Endowment for Financial Education.* <http://www.
collegesummit.org/nefe/pages/section2.html> (5 July
2006).

University of Texas Southwest Medical Center at Dallas. "The
Freshman Fifteen" *annecollins.com.* Available from http://
www.annecollins.com/diet-news/freshman-fifteen.htm.
Internet. Accessed 5 July 2006.

Wellington, Terra. "Financial Stress Ends With Simple
Changes" [Article, June 16, 2003]. *SunCoach:
Your Wellness Guide.* Available from http://www.
terrawellington.com/Column2003/061603.htm. Internet.
Accessed 5 July 2006.

Worthington, Janet Farrar and Farrar, Ronald. *The Ultimate
College Survival Guide* (4th Ed.). New Jersey: Peterson's,
1998.

about the authors

Rich Holly

Rich Holly is the Dean of the College of Visual and Performing Arts at Northern Illinois University, one of the most celebrated and comprehensive arts colleges in the United States. He has been a professor of music for more than thirty years, and has served as an academic advisor continuously throughout his career in higher education. As an author and composer he has over one hundred fifty publications in his name, and he is the author of *Majoring in Music: All the Stuff You Need to Know.* As a percussionist, Rich has performed with several major symphony orchestras and as the drummer for numerous jazz and pop music luminaries. Rich has numerous recording credits as both a performer and producer, and he has performed and presented workshops throughout North America, Central America, Europe and Asia. Rich serves as an arts advisor to various city and regional governments in addition to serving as a consultant for noted non-profit arts agencies and organizations. During the years 2005 and 2006 he served as President of the Percussive Arts Society, and he remains a frequent guest speaker providing motivational and leadership clinics and workshops to music students.

Lemuel Watson

Dr. Lemuel W. Watson is Professor and Executive Director of the Center for P–20 Engagement at Northern Illinois

University. He is the former Dean of the College of Education at Northern Illinois University and the former Dean for the division of Academic Support at Heartland College. He completed his graduate work at Indiana University in Bloomington, Indiana. His career spans across various divisions in higher education, faculty and administration, and public policy. He has numerous experiences in all types of institutions, including public, private, and two-year colleges, where he has held faculty and administrative positions. Dr. Watson has been a Senior Research Fellow at the C. Houston Center at Clemson University and Research Fellow at the Institute for Southern Studies at University of South Carolina. He is a Fulbright Scholar and has written articles, books, and served as editor for several volumes related to organizational behavior, educational leadership and administration, human development, public policy and higher education. He has provided workshops and professional development opportunities to executives, teachers, and administrators in the United States as well as abroad including countries such as Thailand, Philippines, Belarus, China, and Mexico. He serves on a number of professional organizational executive boards and is a member of the Board of Visitors for the National Defense University in Washington, D.C. He is a Certified Master Coach by the Behavioral Coaching Institute of Sydney, Australia and a Certified Trainer through the Center for Entrepreneurial Resources at Ball State University at Muncie, Indiana. He worked as the Coordinator of Continuing Education for the Small Business Development Center in The Darla Moore College of Business at the University of South Carolina. In addition, he is a Certified Systems Engineer by Electronic Data Systems Corporation (EDS) of Plano, Texas. During 2010-2011 he was awarded the U.S. Embassy Policy Specialist (EPS) fellowship by the International Research and Exchanges Board of the U.S. Department of State. He continues to provide training and professional development throughout the globe as a consultant and speaker.